Read This Bef
You Start This

1. This book is designed to inspire, not to inform.

Your brain is limited in terms of how much information it can absorb and process. Once this limit is exceeded, your brain becomes overloaded and over-stressed. If this state is not resolved, it can eventually lead to a decline in both your physical and mental health.

It's very likely that what you actually need is not more information, but rather more inspiration. Once inspired, you will take the vital action required for you to achieve your personal and professional goals. This, in turn, will inspire you to connect with like-minded others, who will help you however and whenever they can.

By harnessing the incredible power of community, you will quickly discover that while there will always be lots of effort involved, the method by which you will achieve all of your goals is actually very simple and involves lots of fun.

2. Theoretical Knowledge
+ Practical Application
= True Knowledge

To quote the great Johann Wolfgang von Goethe:

"Knowing is not enough; we must apply.
  Willing is not enough; we must do."

The main aim of this book is to inspire you to focus on activities which will not only enrich your life, but will also teach you invaluable true knowledge in the process.

3. This book is no longer than is necessary.

In recent years, much has been written about the average reader's shrinking attention span. Much of this is due to the non-stop news cycle and round-the-clock social media grossly accelerating our consumption habits. These same habits have also influenced our book reading habits. As recently as 2011, for example, the average book length of the #1 non-fiction bestseller was 467 pages. By 2017, however, that number had plummeted to just 273 pages.

There is absolutely no 'fluff' or 'padding' contained within this book. By that, I mean I haven't included any extra pages just for the sake of making the book longer. The world is full of unfinished books and I want to ensure that this will *not* be one of them. Instead, I want this book to be one which inspires <u>action</u>. No book, however brilliant, can ever be truly life-changing if the information contained within it is not put into action.

Also, I've deliberately broken up long paragraphs into smaller chunks of text. My priority is to help make this book easy to read, *not* to win any literary awards. This is why I've often taken many liberties when it comes to grammar, punctuation and my overall writing style. All that matters is that everything in this book is easy to understand and even easier to apply.

4. You will write your own version of this book.

Think of this book as the introduction to your *own* book. The suggested activities I recommend are simply my own personal preferences. These serve to help me explain the principles contained in each section.

Feel free to choose your own activities. I strongly encourage you to document your progress from the very start through blogs and vlogs. Use them to connect with others and become the best possible version of yourself while you do so.

As you evolve, so too will this book. My wish is for you to achieve amazing results and eventually contribute to later editions. By sharing your success, you will help to inspire others to use the principles to achieve *their* own goals.

Finally, there are no chapters in The Connection Code. While it can be divided into 6 main sections, my hope is that you read it all in one sitting. This is because I want this book to serve as a catalyst, inspiring you to take immediate action and get the results in life you both want and deserve.

Thanks for reading and I look forward to hearing about your success!

Paul Hurley
March 2020

The Case For Connection

Are you "successful" yet dissatisfied with your life?

One of the great ironies of the modern age is that many people can be very rich in terms of money, yet extremely *poor* when it comes to love, happiness and their overall enjoyment of life.

How can this be?

We are currently at a critical point in human history. More than ever before, the decisions and actions of those in power are been driven almost exclusively by male energy. So-called "leaders" impatiently and aggressively seek to control others through spreading ignorance and fear through the might of the media.

Consequently, many of us have lost touch with our ability to access our nurturing feminine energy, which enables creativity, tranquility and simply being. As a result of this vital energy being stifled, the result is a world which is totally out of balance and harmony.

Modern society has often conditioned many people into doing what they *think* will make them happy, only for them to soon discover that it is actually making them miserable, lonely and disillusioned with life itself. The end result is more depression, dysfunction and addiction than has ever existed before.

The Root Cause Is Disconnection

Unless you are connected to your purpose, you will find it impossible to truly connect with others and achieve the level of mental, physical and spiritual fulfilment you both desire and deserve.

Technology is a big part of the problem, but also a big part of the *solution*. The chronic misuse of iPhones, for example, has resulted in a serious disruption to the family unit. Whereas children, parents and grandparents used to openly communicate and interact with each other, the current generation is now spending more of its time interacting with technology than with other human beings. This creates disconnection, which causes isolation, which will ultimately lead to despair, depression and deep unhappiness in life.

But what if we were to use modern technology to speed up the connection with others? What if we were to use it to communicate, create and collaborate with like-minded people located all across the world?

While technology can provide us with the speed of connection we require, how do we best *deepen* our connection with each other?

The answer to this vital question is provided by nature and is found in our prehistoric past.

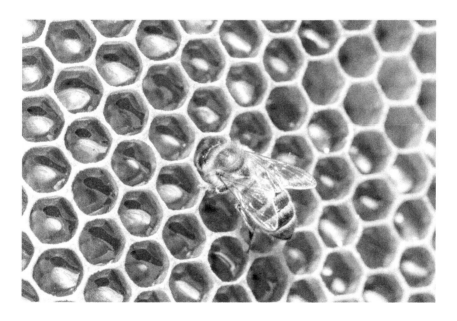

The Power Of The Hexagon

For over 100 million years, bees have built their hives using hexagons. They do so for two main reasons.

Firstly, the hexagon structure of each honeycomb cell enables the bees to fill it with a maximum amount of honey, whilst simultaneously using as little precious wax as possible.

Secondly, and equally importantly, every hexagonal cell fits tightly with every other cell, like the easiest jigsaw puzzle imaginable.

Because of this, the bees are able to work together collectively, simultaneously and constantly to achieve a mutual objective.

Scientists widely agree that bees instinctively "know" to build hexagon-shaped cells for their honeycombs because it is wired into their DNA.

Ask yourself this question

What if the ability to connect with each other and work together was similarly wired into the DNA of all human beings too?

The 6 Dimensions Of Wellness Are:

1. Physical
2. Emotional
3. Intellectual
4. Spiritual
5. Vocational
6. Social

The 6 Age Stages Of Life Throughout Life Are:

1. Infancy
2. Childhood
3. Adolescence
4. Early Adulthood
5. Middle Adulthood
6. Late Adulthood

6 Degrees Of Separation vs 6 Degrees Of Connection

Six degrees of separation is the concept that all people are six, or fewer, social connections away from each other. According to this theory, any two people can be connected in a maximum of six steps, due to a chain of "a friend of a friend" introductions.

This is usually illustrated in a parallel diagram:

SIX DEGREES OF SEPARATION

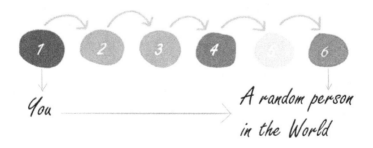

You → A random person in the World

Note that there is only a direct connection between each consecutive degree, but *not* to the other four degrees. For example, the 1st degree is directly connected to the 2nd, but is not directly connected to the 3rd, 4th, 5th or 6th degrees. As a result, the depth of these connections is inevitably non-existent.

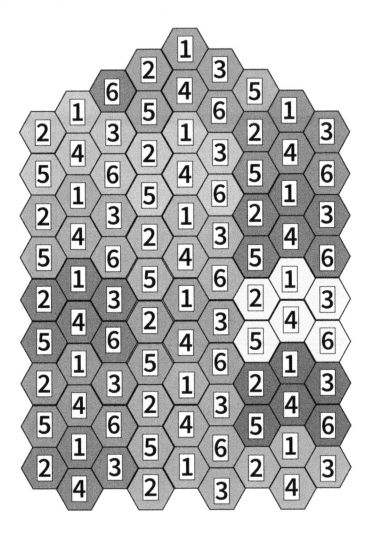

Notice how each of the 6 connections is directly connected to each other.

Imagine human connection worked exactly like a bee hive in terms of activity and interaction.

Imagine if everyone within a community helped everyone else fully develop each of the 6 dimensions of wellness......

Imagine if this community connected with everyone within the 6 age stages to help them all throughout life......

<u>This</u> is what The Connection Code is all about.

Why Connection Is The Key

While bees have existed for over 100 million years, the first human tribe only emerged 100,000 years ago. Members of indigenous tribes, however, have always worked together to help each other in a very similar way to bees. They still do. Why? Because it is exactly the way in which human beings were designed to co-exist.

In the Western World, especially, we largely behave in an isolated, non-tribal way. <u>This</u> is the root cause of disconnection and all the related side-effects: depression, dysfunction and addiction.

There is a dream you have always had inside you, ever since you were very young. It is that inner voice, telling you what you *really* should be doing. Only fear has prevented you from sharing your dream with others and putting the required amount of energy into pursuing and achieving it. It is very likely that you've ignored that dream after being told to "grow up" or "be realistic". It doesn't ever have to be this way.

This book outlines a philosophy which, once implemented, will help improve your sense of well-being. It will also rekindle your innate ability to easily connect with others. Once you realise that you are "enough" exactly the way you *already* are, you can then focus on doing what you love, developing your strengths, and becoming the very best version of yourself. As a result, you will become someone who is of great help to others.

This will lead to you being highly valued by a community of like-minded people, each of whom will be delighted to use their unique skills and strengths to help you whenever and however they can. As part of a supportive and interactive community, you will be able to form deep connections, valued friendships and even build profitable businesses together.

The key to the Connection Code philosophy is to firstly connect with your purpose and, secondly, connect with others in the process. By using technology in the best possible way, you will establish deep and meaningful friendships with amazing men and women all over the world. In addition, you can also use the mass collaboration philosophy of Open Source to help develop and build businesses together with others within your community. This book will outline a method by which you can use your unique gifts to help others and help yourself too.

My Story

Both depression and connection have been huge parts of my life for as long as I can remember.

While I believe it's essentially impossible to consciously identify the exact time at which I started feeling "depressed", I would say it started when I was 12. I did very well in primary school and really enjoyed it. When I entered secondary school, however, things changed dramatically. I had chosen to join a German secondary school, based entirely on the fact that my cousin (and best friend) attended there.

Shortly after starting school there, I quickly found out that my new school had little to no regard for the Irish language. This just so happened to be my favourite subject in primary school. My new class was full of students constantly protesting as to why they needed to study the only subject at which I ever excelled.

Not a good start.

Suddenly, school seemed less about learning and more about doing well at exams. Doing well in exams was achieved not by me being creative, but instead as a reward for essentially giving back the exact answers my teachers *told* me to give them. The more I complied and did what I was told, the more I would be rewarded with good grades. This was not for me. I felt totally out of place in this environment, lacked interest in any of the subjects and found it absolutely impossible to concentrate during class.

Needless to say, I did not do well in exams. Each year, my results got worse and worse. I was given the nickname "Failure" by someone in my class who excelled in school. This had a devastating effect on me, mainly because it reflected how I felt about myself at the time. In such an environment, my entire sense of self-esteem became directly linked to how well I did at school. The worse I did at school, the worse I felt about myself. The worse I felt about myself, the worse I did at school. The downward spiral of depression continued until I hit rock bottom at the age of 19 and no longer wanted to live. After hearing about the suicide of a childhood friend of mine, I was shocked into taking action. I immersed myself in all the philosophy, psychology and self-help books I could find. Applying every theory and technique contained within each of them, I quickly found out what worked and what didn't. My hope is that reading this book will help you progress in life, whilst sparing you the arduous and time-consuming trial and error I endured along the way.

The Antidote To Depression

Everyone who has ever suffered from depression has their own unique story. Not everyone has a similar experience to mine. Depression can take many forms and people can endure various different types of traumatic experiences, which contribute to the development of their depression. Nevertheless, I believe the solution is still the same no matter what the cause.

As simplistic as this may seem, I consider depression to be a symptom of disconnection. Once viewed in this way, the logical solution to depression is connection.

It has taken me over 20 years of in-depth research and painful life experience to reach this conclusion. Despite this, I believe it is important for me to point out that I am very <u>grateful</u> for having suffered years of depression. While I would not wish it on my worst enemy, my experience has provided me with both the understanding and compassion required to greatly help people who are currently feeling trapped by depression.

What made me so sensitive to depression also made me sensitive to the well-being of others. Without the experience of having once felt utterly disconnected myself, it would have been impossible for me to genuinely and authentically write about connection and how to best achieve it with others.

Regardless of your wants and needs on a personal or professional level, connection is always going to be the key to making <u>everything</u> happen.

Your Story

Over the last decade, the most successful films have come from the Marvel and Star Wars franchises. Despite originating in the 60s and 70s, these stories have proven to be hugely relevant to successive generations. There is a very good reason for the seemingly everlasting popularity of these movies. This is because stories about heroes are metaphors for the challenges we all face throughout life.

For example, consider the story of Luke Skywalker, the hero in Star Wars. Experiencing tragedy at a very young age, he is forced to set out on an exciting, though often dangerous journey in life. Rather than being ruined by the trauma of his early experiences, however, he instead develops new strength and wisdom. In the process, he finds meaning and fulfilment in life. The same is true for Peter Parker, who goes on to become Spiderman.

Just like the heroes we see in movies, ordinary people all possess the power to live lives which are every bit as dramatic and worthy. Very often, their own stories involve overcoming *far* more traumatic experiences and events than any "superhero" could ever possibly encounter.

The Adversity Advantage

While it is natural to wish for a life filled with pleasure, it is essential that you recognise adversity as an inescapable part of life. Not only that, it frequently serves to drive people to take on the challenges required for them to achieve extraordinary results.

It is inevitable that you will face difficult events, or even tragedies, throughout your life. While you can obviously never change what has happened in the past, you can always change how you choose to deal with it.

Together with crucial learnings and insights, adversity can also awaken you to a life filled with meaning. This is only possible, however, by focusing on, understanding and deliberately taking control of how you think and behave every day. Doing so will enable you to overcome adversity so you can move forward and live the life you want and deserve.

It is trauma which triggers within you the need to tell your story. It also helps you understand painful experiences, which have had massive effects on your life. As you struggle to make sense of what you have experienced, this is where transformation and growth occurs.

The Philosophy Of Well Being

There are two very different philosophical traditions to the study of well-being:

1. Eudaimonism

Dating back to Aristotle, this was a central concept in his overall philosophy. While it is a Greek word commonly translated as happiness, it is widely considered that a more accurate translation is actually "human flourishing or prosperity".

According to Aristotle, Eudaimonia was used as the term for the highest human good. It involves a lifelong pursuit of seeking meaning, overcoming the existential challenges of life, and actualising human potential.

2. Hedonism

By contrast, this is the philosophy that the main goal of life is to instead seek pleasure as a result of maintaining proper control over both adversity and prosperity.

It dates back to Aristippus, the founder of the Cyrenaic school of philosophy. Although a pupil of Socrates, he went on to adopt a very different philosophical outlook. Unlike his great master, Arisippus advocated a life dedicated to seeking pleasure, happiness and enjoyment.

Needless to say, both philosophies couldn't be more different from each other. It is not a matter, however, of choosing one over the other. The Roman philosopher Epicurus advocated seeking an ideal balance between the two, a life which would encompass both virtue and pleasure.

With this in mind, consider the way in which Western society has operated over the last few decades. It is immediately clear that an equal balance does not exist at all. Hedonism is clearly favoured at the expense of eudaimonism. For example, we all intrinsically *know* that friendships and relationships are much more important than fame or status. Yet the masses lead lives that are entirely inconsistent with this belief.

Just look at the millions of men and women on Facebook and Instagram, all seeking the approval of absolute strangers in the form of 'likes' and 'followers'. Many others behave in the same way in their hedonistic pursuits of money, possessions and status. It could be argued that there is nothing wrong with any of this. However, society undeniably suffers as a whole when people are not equally engaged in their pursuit of personal growth, intimacy and contributions to the community.

According to the philsopher John Stuart Mill, the only people who are happy are those who "have their minds fixed on some object other than their own happiness; on the happiness of others, on the improvement of mankind, even on some art or pursuit, followed not as a means, but as itself an ideal end." When everyone follows the same 'paying it forward' philosophy, it is possible to achieve the best of <u>both</u> worlds. Hedonic well-being is actually a by-product of the achievement of eudaimonic well-being. The key is to first provide value to others and then reap the rewards as a result of doing so.

Imagine the story of your life in the form of a movie, with you cast as the hero on your own life journey. While you are the lead character, the 'movie' that is your life will inevitably involve other characters too. Some will play significant roles, while others will play cameos and mere bit parts. Be aware, of course, that *you* will play similar roles in the lives of others. Ultimately, long-term happiness is achieved by connecting with others and helping them on their journeys while you are on your journey.

To get the very most out of life, you will need to fully optimise your ability to connect with others and also connect meanings and understandings to the experiences and events you encounter throughout your journey. My aim with this book is to provide you with the blueprint for you to achieve exactly this.

Physical

From the moment it was launched back in 2005, YouTube changed the world forever. Suddenly, it was easy to immediately access incredible information of all types in the form of free videos. Today, an astonishing 300 hours of video are uploaded to YouTube every single minute. While there are countless hours of amazing content about how to improve your physical health and wellness, obesity still remains a major problem. In addition, more people have diabetes than ever before in human history. With so much information being freely available, how can this have happened?

As weird as it may initially sound, I believe that having access to unlimited information is actually a big part of the problem. Many men and women become so distracted by having so many possible options available, they never actually decide on choosing and implementing a single one of them. Consequently, they don't take the necessary action required to get the results they want.

With this in mind, I've restricted this section to a few key concepts, together with some recommended habits. They are easy to apply, yet yield fantastic results.

Is Sitting Really The New Smoking?

In recent years, sitting has been branded the "new smoking" due to the health risks it supposedly causes, particularly for those with sedentary office jobs. All of a sudden, the simple act of sitting has been linked with the onset of cancer, heart disease, diabetes and even depression. Many companies have responded to these claims, going so far as to install standing desks in their offices for their employees.

But is sitting *really* that bad for your health?

The truth of the matter is that not all sitting is equal. For example, sitting down at work isn't strongly linked with serious long-term health risks. One of the reasons for this may be because higher status jobs involve more sitting, and higher socioeconomic position is associated with a lower risk of chronic disease. Sitting watching TV, on the other hand, has been consistently linked with long-term health risks including heart disease and type 2 diabetes. Those who watch a lot of TV every day, for instance, generally tend to be of a lower socioeconomic status and unemployed. As a result, they are constantly exposed to unhealthy food advertising, which greatly influences them to make poor meal choices.

Each of these factors significantly increases the likelihood of poor physical and mental health. Yet while these TV studies may demonstrate that excessive TV viewing is bad for our health, they tell us absolutely nothing about the health risks of sitting.

Instead of demonising sitting and listening to the outrageous claims made by the media, it is wiser to consider the much wider problem of physical inactivity. This has long been proven to be the *real* cause of long-term health risks. The first priority, therefore, is as simple as it is blindingly obvious: increase the amount of physical activity you perform every day and reap the many health rewards as a result of doing so.

Walking sadly remains a much underused and unappreciated tool for achieving optimum wellness. Many argue that since we do it so frequently on a daily basis, the body does not respond to it by getting fitter and stronger. However, such people are missing out on the many benefits that walking provides. Any calories burnt or fitness results produced are nothing more than a nice bonus.

The *real* benefit of walking is that it greatly helps decrease your stress levels. It does so by removing you from the situations and environments which typically trigger stressful feelings within you. Decreasing your stress levels helps reduce the amount of cortisol released in your body. Known as "the stress hormone", the effects of too much cortisol in the body include impaired cognitive performance, suppressed thyroid function, higher blood pressure and increased abdominal fat.

Outdoor walking is a wonderful way of decreasing stress. While you are enjoying a brisk walk in a park, for example, your thoughts will drift away and your mind will be able to relax and wander to wherever it wants. It's very similar to what happens during meditation. Your conscious mind is disengaged and all your worries and concerns are put on hold. When you return to deal with them, you will do so in a much more resourceful state. So use walking to help you control stress before stress controls *you.*

Strength: Your Most Vital Possession

Past the age of 25, both males and females lose between half a pound to a full pound of muscle every year. This has a noticeable effect on the strength of an individual. You are unable to do things as easily as before. The majority of people casually, yet regretfully, attribute this to "ageing".

Muscle loss has an even more devastating effect on your body composition. This is because muscle tissue is the most metabolically expensive tissue you have. It takes between 50 to 100 calories a day just to maintain a single pound of muscle. If, for example, a 35 year old female has lost 8 pounds of muscle in the last decade, she will no longer be burning the 800 calories a day that she did when she was 25. If she eats the same way she did 10 years ago, therefore, she is likely to have gained a considerable amount of excess weight in the form of fat.

This is why you can often gain weight without making any change whatsoever in the way you eat. The cause is not actually ageing, but rather muscle loss. You have simply neglected to keep the lean tissue you had when you were younger. Therefore, strength training is vitally important for males and females of all ages. In fact, the older you get, the more important strength training becomes.

Greasing The Groove

The idiomatic phrase 'practice makes perfect' is often used to encourage and motivate someone to keep practising. The theory is that it is possible to learn something or develop a skill if you practise enough. Talent, it is claimed, is a result of thousands of hours of purposeful practice, not any innate talent. Those who believe that attaining excellence hinges on talent, on the other hand, are much more likely to give up if they show insufficient early promise at a particular skill.

If you play sports and adopt the "practice makes perfect" mantra, you will accept that your success will largely be determined by the amount of time and effort you spend developing the skills required to excel at your chosen sport. To become a better football player, therefore, you have to practise football. To become a better tennis player, you must practice tennis.

If this seems all too obvious, consider that to become stronger, you have to practise strength. It is unlikely you have ever thought of strength as something to be practised, but it is indeed true. Like any other skill, it requires consistent and dedicated work.

The Muscle-Neuron Connection

Whenever you put your muscles under stress, they immediately react by contracting. This is initiated by your nervous system sending a signal to your muscle fibres. When you repeatedly perform a particular movement, the muscle fibres involved receive an identical signal over and over again. The human body is naturally designed to constantly adapt to new stresses. Because of this, it quickly develops a more efficient neuromuscular motor pattern. This makes it easier and far less stressful to perform the same task next time.

This process is called myelination and is how your body responds to the regular practice of a specific movement. A fatty white substance develops a sheath around the axons of nerve cells. This helps speed up the ability of nerve impulses to move through your muscles. The quicker your nerve cells can fire, the quicker your muscles can contract.

Not only does improving the efficiency of neuromuscular motor patterns make movements easier to perform, it also provides you with more potential force to best perform the movements. As a result, you are able to recruit a greater number of muscle fibres that contract. As a result, you're able to exert more force, becoming stronger in the process.

No Pain, Lots of Gain!

There are two main ways to get strong. The first involves you lifting progressively heavier weights, usually to the point where you cannot perform another repetition. This is called "training until failure". This type of training causes micro trauma (tiny tears) in the muscle fibres. As they recover, they respond to the stress caused and rebuild stronger than before. This is the most popular form of training.

The second way is less known but is gradually gaining popularity due to the pioneering work of Pavel Tsatsouline. A Belarusian fitness instructor, Tsatsouline is most notable for popularising the kettlebell in the modern era in the West.

Known as "greasing the groove", it is a training principle used to develop neurological pathways, increase strength and improve your ability to perform a specific exercise. It involves practicing the exercise using multiple sets, but with a very low number of repetitions. This is to ensure that the muscles involved in the exercise are never pushed to the point of exhaustion.

Tsatsouline claims that training to failure is not only unnecessary, but is actually *counterproductive*. If your body fails to perform the next repetition of an exercise, he believes, the groove will get 'rusty'. Despite all your strenuous efforts, your muscles actually end up contracting weaker than before.

Simply put - *If you are training to failure, you are training to fail.*

Get Into The Groove!

Pick some exercises in which you want to become stronger. I recommend you select bodyweight exercises like pull-ups, push-ups, and squats because they are much easier to perform on a regular basis than dumbbell and barbell exercises.

There's no fixed recommendation for how many sets of each exercise you should do. Instead, perform them as often as possible throughout the day.

Let's say right now you can do 10 push-ups. You would start off doing 40% of that, or 4 reps. 5 sets of 4 reps would mean a total of 20 push-ups every day. Every two weeks, you could add another rep to your sets. After one month, therefore, you would be up to 30 push-ups a day.

If you feel fatigued at the end of your sets, this is a sign that you're moving too quickly. As long as you avoid pushing yourself to muscular failure, however, it is unlikely that you'll feel tired or over-trained. Instead, you should feel stronger.

Your first goal is to make greasing the groove a habit, something that is simply part of your daily routine. The best way to achieve this is by setting alarms in your phone throughout the day, each of which act as reminder signals for you to perform a set of repetitions. After a few weeks of doing this every day, you will be doing this without thinking too much about it.

It's essential that you focus on maintaining impeccable form when performing the exercises. Doing so ensures you "program" the movement into your neuromuscular system as well as possible. One of the reasons to avoid training until failure is that your form suffers greatly whenever you become overly fatigued. As you progress, you can add additional resistance by using either a weight belt or weighted vest. Rather than help you build big muscles, the focus of greasing the groove is the development of specific muscle strength, skill and expertise of a movement. While it requires dedicated and consistent effort, it creates fantastic results. Best of all, the exercises can be performed anywhere and at any time. If you are not getting the results you want via exhausting workouts, give "greasing the groove" a go. Your body will quickly show its appreciation in the form of increased strength and improved physical performance.

Get Cold To Burn Fat!

Human beings are essentially creatures of comfort. This is especially the case when it comes to heat. At all times, we seek out ways to ensure that we remain warm and comfortable whenever possible.

Hot fires, double glazing, insulation, and air conditioning devices are just a few examples of how to maintain the temperature you like wherever you are. When the weather is cold, we wear coats, scarves, hats, gloves and thick socks. All of this undoubtedly makes it less stressful for the body. This seems like a very sensible thing to do, yet can lead to you missing out on a multitude of physical benefits.

Instead of avoiding it all costs, you can actually use the cold to improve your health. In many parts of Scandinavia, for example, ice-hole swimming is popular. This involves swimmers carving a hole in the ice and then immersing themselves in freezing cold water. It is very likely that reading that last sentence caused you to shiver, as you questioned the sanity of people who willingly and regularly engage in such an activity. With this in mind, I will explain the method behind their "madness".

So why exactly is exposure to cold so beneficial? It all begins with your blood vessels. Your body contains a whopping 125,000 km (77,671 miles) of blood vessels, enough to go around the world three times. Their function is to ensure that enough amounts of nutrients and oxygen are continually delivered to the billions of cells in your body. Simply put: the better your blood vessels work, the better your entire body will work.

If you take a cold shower, for example, your body will respond to the stimulus by immediately restricting blood flow to the less vital areas of your body.

It does so to prevent your body temperature falling below 35°C (95°F). Your body will therefore prioritise your heart and vital organs ahead of other body areas. Examples would include your fingers and toes, which are not actually crucial for your survival. For this reason, these areas typically go numb much quicker than any other areas of the body when subjected to cold temperatures. Once the body warms up again, however, the blood vessels dilate and the circulation to these areas returns to normal once again. In the same way that weight training strengthens your muscles by exposing them to stress, you can strengthen your blood vessels and improve your circulation with cold exposure training.

In recent years, there has been a huge change in the understanding of fat and its role in nutrition and human health. Whereas it was once considered a substance to be avoided at all costs, nutrition experts now acknowledge that dietary fat plays a vital role in maintaining well-being.

These days, most people are aware that not all fat is created equal. There are "good fats" and "bad fats". The former contain essential fatty acids. As their name suggests, they are literally essential for your health.

That's not where the differentiation ends though. What you may not know is that the fat in your body is actually made up of different colours. Scientists have identified two main types of fat—brown and white— which play very different roles within the body.

1. <u>White fat</u> - This is the type of fat you've most likely known about your entire life. It stores your excess energy in the form of large fat droplets. These accumulate around various parts of your body, especially your "problem areas". This fat protects your organs and also helps keep you warm by providing insulation for your body. Having too much abdominal white fat, however, has long been linked with the onset of heart disease, diabetes, and many other metabolic diseases.

2. <u>Brown fat</u> - This type of fat stores energy in a smaller space than white fat. Its colour is due to it being packed full of iron-rich mitochondria. When brown fat burns, it produces heat without shivering. Referred to as thermogenesis, this process involves the brown fat burning calories. Because of this, brown fat is now being widely touted as a possible treatment for obesity. Scientists have recently worked out how the body can convert its stores of white fat into brown fat.

Babies are born with rich stores of brown fat, approximately 5% of their total body mass. This is referred to as "constitutive" brown fat. Located on their upper spine and shoulders, it helps keep them warm. Although it was previously believed that all brown fat disappeared with age, it has now been established that adults also store small reserves in the shoulder and neck areas. That is not the most interesting recent discovery however.

Scientists have also identified another type of fat, which is referred to as being "recruitable". Located in muscles and white fat throughout the body, it can be transformed into brown fat under the right circumstances. Cold training is widely considered to be the very best way to help your body to recruit more brown cells.

In addition to helping reduce body fat, cold water training has also been linked to the following health benefits:

Reduced Stress Levels: The stress of regularly taking cold showers stimulates a process called hardening. This involves your nervous system gradually becoming accustomed to coping with moderate levels of stress. As you develop your ability to handle stress, you are able to remain relaxed and composed the next time you experience a stressful situation.

Increased Immune Strength: Recent scientific research has demonstrated that taking cold showers increases the amount of white blood cells in your body. The role of these blood cells is to protect your body against disease. By increasing your metabolic rate, scientists believe that regular cold water exposure stimulates this immune response.

Increased Mental Strength: My own personal approach is to take a cold shower first thing in the morning, shortly after getting out of bed. I do this simply because it is the very *last* thing I feel like doing, especially immediately after spending hours asleep in a warm and comfortable bed. Consistently and deliberately doing the exact opposite of what is comfortable develops incredible discipline and willpower. It will also help set you apart from others, who wilt and crumble when faced with the very first sign of discomfort and adversity.

The very best thing about cold training is that it costs no money whatsoever. To get started, simply take a regular hot shower and turn on the cold tap for the last 30 seconds. Despite the fact that every part of you will try to convince you *not* to do it, overcoming this fear will provide you with rewards that go far beyond just the physical benefits. When you take your first cold shower, you will immediately realise that the fear of taking one is infinitely more unpleasant than the actual feeling of the cold water itself.

In addition to the physical benefits, you will also find that the habit of taking cold showers helps you build self-discipline. Developing the ability to consciously embrace discomfort will help you attain a level of mental strength, which will help you in every area of life. Until you've taken one, you will find it hard to believe how invigorating cold showers really are. With repeated practice, however, your mind will soon associate pleasure with taking them. They truly have a positive and profound effect on your sense of well-being.

Emotional

When most people think about making dietary changes, it is usually motivated by the desire to improve the way they look on the outside. Their main motivation is to change their body shape. They achieve this by losing excess body fat and/or gaining more lean body tissue (muscle). While I certainly recommend doing so to everyone, this is absolutely not enough by itself to ensure your optimum physical health, let alone your optimum *emotional* health.

Are You Getting Enough Of This Vital Hormone?

Whenever the subject of hormones is discussed, the first ones that tend to come to mind are usually testosterone, oestrogen and insulin. Yet, there are some 50 different hormones secreted and circulated within the human body. Their function is to communicate between organs and tissues for physiological regulation and behavioural activities. These include digestion, metabolism, respiration, tissue function, sensory perception, sleep, excretion, lactation, stress induction, growth and development, movement, reproduction, and mood manipulation. Needless to say, therefore, hormones have a huge effect on both our physical and mental health.

Yet there is one crucial hormone that the vast majority of people lack in the amount required by their bodies in order to be healthy. The sad truth is that few people are even aware of it in the first place. "What is this 'secret hormone'?", I hear you ask. The answer will both surprise and confuse you: Vitamin D.

Vitamin D is very different from other vitamins such as Vitamins A, B, C, E and K. These vitamins are required for human health, but are not produced by the body. Vitamin D, on the other hand, is formed *in* the body. It functions as a chemical messenger, just like your sex and adrenal hormones. This is why it is considered a hormone instead of a vitamin.

Recent studies have demonstrated that it helps protect against the following diseases linked with low Vitamin D:

- Cancer
- Cardiovascular disease

- Hypertension
- Diabetes
- Multiple sclerosis
- Rheumatoid arthritis
- Inflammatory bowel disease
- Autoimmune diseases
- Chronic pain
- Influenza.

Yet scientists are currently most fascinated with the numerous studies regarding mental health and depression.

Are You SAD?

Seasonal affective disorder (SAD) is a type of medical depression that occurs at a certain time of the year, normally in winter. It is believed that shorter days and less daylight may trigger a chemical alteration in the brain, causing symptoms of depression.

SAD is believed to be caused by shorter days, which provide insufficient amounts of sunlight. This has been linked to a chemical modification in the brain, which is associated with many symptoms of depression. If you live in a place with long winter nights, you are therefore at an increased danger of developing SAD.

Scientists have also observed a direct correlation between SAD and the production of melatonin, a sleep-linked hormone. During the shorter and darker days of winter, the body manufactures more melatonin. Light and darkness also control your biological clock, or circadian rhythm, which impacts hormones that regulate your appetite and metabolism. This is what causes those with SAD to gain weight.

There are two forms of SAD:

1. Fall-onset

Known as "winter depression", symptoms start in the late autumn to early winter months. They become less frequent during the summer months.

2. Spring-onset

A much less frequent type of SAD, this is also known as "summer depression." Its symptoms begin in late spring to early summer, slowly increasing in the late autumn and winter months.

Symptoms are often similar to other types of depression and typically include the following:

1. A feeling of hopelessness
2. Increased appetite with weight gain
3. Increased sleep and daytime drowsiness
4. Decreased energy and ability to concentrate
5. Loss of interest in work and pleasure in activities previously enjoyed
6. Sluggish movements
7. Social withdrawal
8. Irritability and anxiety
9. Headaches
10. Reduced ability to focus or concentrate
11. Fatigue or low energy level
12. Diminished sex drive

Besides chronic depression, Vitamin D deficiency has long been associated with Seasonal Affective Disorder (SAD). For example, British National Diet and Nutrition surveys from 2008/2009 to 2011/2012 demonstrated that 25% of British adults have low Vitamin D status. Statistics from the US are even more worrying. According to Dr. Michael Holick, one of the leading Vitamin D researchers, 50% of the general US population is at risk of Vitamin D deficiency and insufficiency.

Vitamin D promotes the production of serotonin. The amount of serotonin produced is in direct proportion to the amount of bright sunlight the body receives. Serotonin is widely believed to create sensations of happiness, well being and serenity in people. Since Vitamin D receptors can be found pretty much everywhere in the human body, the ways in which it might help improve your mood are innumerable. For example, low testosterone can impair the mood of men and women and Vitamin D helps regulate testosterone levels. It therefore stands to reason that supplementing with Vitamin D should be a priority, especially if you typically suffer from depression during autumn and winter months.

Why Sunshine Is Not Enough By Itself

Since it was misclassified for so long, the importance of Vitamin D has been entirely underestimated. For example, we are all taught as kids about the importance of Vitamin D when it comes to building healthy bones. We learn that it helps prevent diseases such as rickets, osteomalacia and osteoporosis. To make sure we get enough of the vitamin, we are subsequently told to regularly consume lots of dairy produce, including milk and cheese. As long as we do this, we are told, we will get enough Vitamin D. The unfortunate reality, however, is that nothing could be further from the truth. As a result of this erroneous thinking, human health is greatly suffering.

To begin with, our bodies require Vitamin D for much more than just healthy bones. In the recent past, health experts only really considered the role of Vitamin D to be in maintaining skeletal integrity. They therefore only looked for bone diseases when establishing whether or not people were deficient in it. If you didn't display any signs of rickets or osteoporosis, for example, you were not considered to be lacking in Vitamin D. In the past decade, however, medical doctors have discovered that vitamin D has a much greater part in sustaining overall health than was previously believed.

The dairy industry would love to have you believe that you can take care of all your Vitamin D requirements by simply drinking lots of milk, as well as regularly eating eggs and cheese. This is sadly what many people believe and it is consequently a big reason why their health badly suffers.

The fact of the matter is that only about 10% of our Vitamin D actually comes from what we eat. The remaining 90% is meant to be manufactured by your body. When you are exposed to the sun, its ultraviolet B (UVB) rays transform cholesterol stored in the skin into Vitamin D3. This is by far the most active form of Vitamin D. Receptors for Vitamin D3 are found in almost all the cells of your body. As a steroid hormone, it controls over 1,000 different physiological processes inside of your body. It is absolutely vital for optimum health.

Over the last 20 years, unfortunately, deficiency in Vitamin D3 has been on the rise. While it would be ideal to obtain the majority of their Vitamin D3 from sunlight, people living in

Northern latitudes cannot manufacture sufficient amounts during the winter months.

Experts also believe the following factors have contributed to this deficiency:

1. People today spend much less time outdoors than they did in the past.

2. When people *do* spend time in the sun, they typically wear sunscreen, which blocks UVB radiation. In fact, one study estimated that sunscreen of SPF 30 or more reduces Vitamin D3 production in the body by approximately 95–98%

3. Older people do not manufacture Vitamin D3 from the sun as efficiently as when they were younger. Since people are now living longer, there are more people suffering from a Vitamin D3 deficiency. It is estimated that a 70 year old produces four times less than a 20 year old.

4. There are higher levels of obesity worldwide than ever before. Body fat hinders our ability to use Vitamin D by reducing its bioavailability. Since it is fat soluble, it is stored in that fat. The more body fat you have, the less Vitamin D3 is released into your bloodstream..

What Are The Best Sources Of Vitamin D3?

When sun exposure is insufficient for the manufacture of adequate quantities of it through the skin, it is then necessary to get Vitamin D3 from foods and supplements. Most sources of Vitamin D3 are "fortified" ones, including dairy products such as milk and cheese. Vegetable sources such as mushrooms and yeast contain Vitamin D2, which has only about a third of the biological action of Vitamin D3.

The best food sources of Vitamin D3 are:

i. Oily fish, such as mackerel, salmon, or sardines.
ii. Fish liver oils
iii. Eggs from hens that have been given Vitamin D3.

The easiest and most convenient way to get your required amount is by taking a Vitamin D3 supplement daily. Eat oily fish regularly and expose your skin to sunlight whenever possible. This will ensure that your body is supplied with enough Vitamin D3 every day. Since it is very likely you have been deficient for a long time, expect to see a dramatic transformation in both your energy levels, combined with a noticeable improvement in your overall sense of well being.

How Much Vitamin D3 Do You Need?

The safe upper limit for Vitamin D3 is:

1,000 to 1,500 IU/day for infants
2,500 to 3,000 IU/day for children 1 - 8 years
4,000 IU/day for adults

Gut Health For Good Health!

"All disease begins within the gut." This was according to Hippocrates, widely considered to be one of the most outstanding figures in the history of medicine. While he claimed this over 2,000 years ago, modern science is increasingly proving that he was exactly correct in what he said.

There are two main reasons why gut health is so important. Firstly, the gut is where you break down all the foods you eat into their key nutrients. If this system isn't working well, this will make it very difficult for your gut to absorb these vital nutrients so that you can repair and rebuild the 100 trillion cells which make up your body. Secondly, 80% of your immune system is located within your digestive system. Your immune system provides your body with vital protection against infection and disease.

In the past 20 years, there have been huge advances in the area of gut microbe research. This has largely been due to technology. Up until 2002, the only method used to identify and characterise gut microbes was to culture them on a petri dish. This never provided an accurate representation of what is in our gut. We now know that about 80% of our gut microbes can't actually be cultured in the first place. With the recent advent of gene sequencing technology, however, it is now possible to identify gut microbes according to their genetic blueprint. Each blueprint is as unique as a fingerprint.

Containing a mind-boggling 100 trillion microbial cells, it is no exaggeration whatsoever to say that the gut is packed full of bacteria. In each human body, there is 2-3kg of gut microbes, containing approximately 1,000 different species. Your big toe represents the amount of DNA in your body which is actually yours. Everything else, more than 99%, is *bacterial* DNA.

When your gut health is poor, you may experience all types of health issues that don't initially seem to be related to your digestion. These symptoms range from headaches, fatigue, depression, weight gain, back pain and frequent colds. Numerous recent studies, however, are linking each of these health issues to poor gut health.

Recent scientific research has proven that there is a genuine connection between the digestive tract and the nervous system. The vagus nerve, the longest of the cranial nerves, controls your inner nerve centre—the parasympathetic nervous system. It carries out a range of vital functions, communicating motor and sensory impulses to every organ in your body. Approximately 90 percent of the fibres in the vagus nerve transmit information from the gut to the brain.

Stimulating the vagus nerve that connects the brain and the gut has been proven to be a very effective way of alleviating depression. In fact, your digestive system makes more neurotransmitters than the brain does. There is therefore a very strong correlation between your gut health and your mental health.

The gastrointestinal system is the largest organ of your immune system and is responsible for digesting and absorbing nutrients from food and also for excreting waste. To give you an indication of how big it is, your gut is the size of a basketball court when spread out.

Within the lining of the small intestine are located more than two-thirds of your body's lymphocytes. A vital part of your immune system, lymphocytes help your body fight bacteria, viruses, and other toxins that make you sick. Your gastrointestinal tract possesses its own nervous system. This is called the Enteric Nervous System (ENS). Since it contains as many nerve cells as your spinal cord, the ENS is often referred to as "The Second Brain". Due to its constant communication with your first brain, it has a massive influence on both your mood and mental function.

As well as this, the wide variety of functions of the digestive system all interact with each other and with the food you eat. This helps regulate your weight, your sleep quality, your energy levels, and your susceptibility to illness.

Depending on your lifestyle choices, your bacterial colonies change for better or for worse. Your diet, together with your use of antibiotics, has a tremendous influence on the state of your internal microbial environment. They will greatly determine how your body feels, the effectiveness of your immune system functions, and also how well you digest and assimilate the food you eat.

Happiness Begins In The Gut!

Considered a natural mood stabilizer, serotonin is a chemical that is believed to regulate anxiety, happiness, and mood. Whilst most associated with the brain, however, 95% of the serotonin found in the body is manufactured by the nervous system. Your gut, therefore, plays a very significant role when it comes to your psychological health.

Serotonin plays an important role in the coordinated movement of food through the gut. Many experts in the area of gut health suggest that disturbed gut function reduces the small intestine's ability to break down protein into amino acids, the building blocks of neurotransmitters. The subsequent decrease in the production of serotonin, they believe, can contribute to the onset of depression. With this in mind, it is perhaps a good idea to think of depression as a symptom of gut dysfunction, *instead* of a serotonin deficiency in the brain.

How To Make Your Gut Healthy

Your ability to deal with stress will greatly determine the health of your gut. Throughout history, the fight-or-flight response has helped protect humans from life-threatening situations. Activated by stress hormones such as cortisol and adrenalin, it triggers a multitude of extreme reactions within the body. An example would be providing the body increased strength and speed in anticipation of fighting or running. While this response serves us well in the short-term, it can cause chronic problems if it happens on a regular basis. In stressful corporate environments, for example, this is unfortunately what happens far too often. This results in a wide range of physical problems. These range from chronic fatigue, insomnia, constipation, neurological issues, and memory problems.

Needless to say, your diet also has a profound impact on your gut health. While different people are more sensitive to certain foods than others, there are 4 main types of food which are common causes of stomach distress:

1. Lectins: These are proteins that bind to carbohydrates. They resist being broken down in the gut, which can cause severe problems during digestion. Symptoms can include nausea, vomiting, and diarrhoea.

2. Gluten: This is a group of proteins, which is present in cereal grains such as barley, rye, and oats. Diseases triggered by gluten include celiac disease (CD), non-celiac gluten sensitivity (NCGS), wheat allergy, gluten ataxia and dermatitis herpetiformis.

3. Lactose: Lactose is a type of sugar found naturally in the milk of most mammals. Up to 70% of people don't produce enough lactase to properly digest the lactose in milk. This can lead to symptoms such as stomach pain, bloating, and gas.

4. Fructose: Also known as fruit sugar, fructose is usually absorbed in the small intestine. For those with fructose intolerance, however, some is transported to the colon, where bacteria ferment the fructose. This leads to hydrogen and methane gases being released, which can lead to severe stomach pain and flatulence.

While working to improve your gut health, it is a good idea to monitor your intake of these 4 food types until you find out which ones you can tolerate and which ones cause distress to your gut.

Food to include

Wild Salmon
Sauerkraut
Apple Cider Vinegar
Bone Broth
Garlic
Onions
Miso
Kefir
Kombucha
Mangoes
Lactose-Free Yogurt
Kimchi
Sprouted Grains
Coconut Oil
Fermented Coffee

Make sure to consume a selection of some of these foods on a regular basis. Your stomach will soon thank you and you can expect to see a very positive improvement in both your mood and overall energy levels.

Intellectual

In order to best manage daily life, it is essential that you develop the ability to consistently make good decisions. The decisions you make determine the actions you take, which ultimately have a massive influence on the results you get. To develop this ability, it's crucial that you optimise your cognitive ability to process learning and solve problems. Doing so enables you to think critically and be flexible in your thinking. This is especially important in stressful circumstances, where having a clear head is vital.

Learning new skills and improving existing skills also creates the potential for establishing mutually beneficial collaborations with others. The simple habit of exchanging knowledge with others greatly cultivates intellectual wellness. While we all do this naturally when we are young children, many of us unfortunately lose touch with this habit. For some reason, adult life just seems to get in the way. Maybe you have a job which involves very long hours. Perhaps all your energy is spent looking after your children. Often, it is a mixture of both. Given the multiple stresses of modern life, it is very easy to lose touch with that innate curiosity, which enabled you to instantly create joy as a child.

The good news is that regardless of your age, this ability is still available to you. It is simply dormant through lack of practice. You just need to reawaken and reactivate it. In terms of your emotional wellness, developing your intellect will also help improve your sense of self-esteem. This is because it is easy to measure and track your progress. When learning a new language, for example, you can work through grade books and exams. These provide you with pinpoint feedback regarding the improvements you've made. They also highlight the areas in which you need to improve.

Lifelong learning is absolutely <u>not</u> a process which is exclusively accessed through schools, colleges and universities. In my own personal experience, for example, I've learned much more since I finished my formal education. I attribute this to many years of consciously investing lots of my time and effort into developing and expanding my intellect. Since I only focus on subjects that interest me, I tap into the curious and inquisitive "inner child" within me. As a result, I learn without even consciously trying. Both babies and young children have a sponge-like ability to "soak up" knowledge and new skills. The only reason we lack this ability as adults is because we lose connection with our sense of curiosity.

Reconnecting with this part of yourself is pivotal to your intellectual growth. This is because it inspires you to try new things and develop an understanding of how you view the relationship between yourself, others and the environment around you.

Concentration - The Key To Success

Concentration can be defined as 'the ability to direct one's thinking in the intended direction'. Concentration is directly linked to learning ability and is regarded as one of the most important senses that human beings possess. With a well developed ability to concentrate fully, you can pick up things more quickly and memorise new information more easily. While everybody has the ability to concentrate, it is very easy to get distracted when your mind is racing from one thing to another. This is especially the case these days.

The combination of mobile phones, text messages and social media channels has resulted in a world full of constant distractions and interruptions. This has a very detrimental effect because it conditions you into experiencing instant gratification at the click of a single button. You get into the habit of instantly expecting a reply to a text message you sent only minutes beforehand. All the information you could ever need is available to you via Internet search engines. The consequence of all of this is that concentration has become somewhat of a 'lost art', a skill which the majority of people have lost. This is because they have basically become slaves to their omnipresent mobile devices.

How To Improve Concentration

The process of developing the ability to fully concentrate is similar to that of any other skill. This means repeated practice each and every day until you have developed enough ability to concentrate fully whenever you need to.

In order to achieve any goal, it is essential that you fully develop your ability to direct your entire concentration towards completing the intended task. The sun provides a perfect analogy to help explain how concentration works. When sun rays are scattered, their heating effect is minimal. If these same sun rays are concentrated solely on one particular source, however, the heat they produce is enormously amplified. Concentration works in exactly the same way. The more you are able to direct and focus it, the more easily and more quickly you can achieve your goals.

Learn To Pay Attention

The ability to pay attention is directly related to concentration and learning. While it may be tempting to take on a few projects all at once, it is much better to instead focus all your efforts on completing one single task at a time. Attempting to take on multiple tasks all at once will inevitably result in your attention levels being scattered and fragmented. You may well tell yourself and others that you can "multitask" without any problems at all. The truth of the matter, however, is that you are ultimately unable to fully concentrate or absorb information. When you are totally focused on a single task or objective, on the other hand, your brain responds in a very positive way. It starts by activating the areas of your brain that are related to the object of your focus. Simultaneously, it shuts down the unrelated areas too. This is the process by which your brain focuses your attention, improves your ability to concentrate, and helps you get the results you want.

Establish An Appropriate Environment

In most cases, it is best to eliminate distractions as much as possible when trying to concentrate. While many people claim that listening to music helps them, I personally find that absolute quiet works best. This is especially the case when I'm writing. The writing process requires me to think, create, write and then evaluate what I've just written. While I adore music, I would find it totally impossible to perform at my very best whilst listening to it. However, you may very well find that music inspires you and helps you maintain your concentration when completing mundane tasks. In this case, use familiar music playlists. This is because hearing new songs will always result in a break in your concentration and focus.

Distractions in the form of television and pinging mobile phones are the very worst culprits when it comes to making it impossible to focus. Avoid them at all costs whenever you are trying to concentrate. In addition, avoid people who constantly engage you in conversation. This is especially difficult when you are surrounded by friends or family members, whose company and conversations you enjoy. When around them, it is often impossible for them *not* to distract you, even if it is with a single innocuous question or remark. That's all it takes to break your concentration and also increase your stress levels too. This is where you need to take full responsibility, apply self-discipline and find a more suitable environment. A public library would be my recommendation. There, you will be surrounded by other people, all of whom require the same peace and quiet you do in order to fully concentrate on *their* tasks.

Control Your Desires

In his classic book "Think And Grow Rich", author Napoleon Hill emphasises the importance of what he calls "sex transmutation". This is whereby you use your sexual energy to fully harness your reserves of imagination, courage, will-power, persistence, and creative ability. Hill claims that these abilities can be used as powerful creative forces to help achieve any goal including, of course, the accumulation of wealth.

To improve your concentration, it is vital to be able to maintain control over your desires. This is *much* easier said than done. Desire has long been known as the hardest appetite for humans to control. Once you master the ability to control your desires, you will find it infinitely easier than before to direct your senses towards achieving your chosen goals. Given the fact that your brain is essentially a goal-seeking machine, this ability will help you improve every single area of your life.

Read Every Day

Another simple yet effective way of improving your concentration is by reading. Your preferred choice of reading material may be a daily newspaper, a self-help book, or a science-fiction novel. Whatever it is, I recommend you keep a journal and note down whatever you have gained or learned from reading the extract.

Do this every time you read and it will enable you to absorb information and new insights in a faster and more permanent manner. Making this an everyday habit will result in you developing a strong concentration power.

Why Chess Is "The Game Of Kings"

Known as "the game of kings", chess was routinely played by rulers of empires and kingdoms. They viewed the game as ideal practice for strategising and forecasting the future moves of their adversaries and enemies.

Here are 3 positive effects of chess on the brain, which are extremely useful in every area of life:

1. It increases your creativity

One four-year study split students from grades 7 to 9 into three groups, to see which activity stimulated the most growth in creative thinking. One group played chess, one used computers, and one did other activities once a week for 32 weeks. At the end of this experiment, it was found that the chess group had scored higher in all measures of creativity, with originality being their biggest area of gain.

2. It improves concentration

Chess demands a level of sustained concentration that no other game requires. Becoming distracted or looking away from the board for even a moment can result in the loss of a match. When you develop the ability to focus your mind, you conserve your energy and don't waste it on irrelevant thoughts or activities. Regularly playing chess will improve your ability to concentrate so that you can be more efficient and take charge of your life.

3. It teaches planning and foresight

The prefrontal cortex is the area of the brain responsible for planning, judgment, and self-control. Being able to control your emotions allows you to avoid making reckless and harmful errors, which are caused by impulsive and reactive actions. Improving your ability to both think and act strategically will greatly help you make better decisions in all areas of life.

Every chess game consists of a series of power struggles. While the ultimate goal is to achieve checkmate, the journey there requires arranging your forces in such a way that you increase the combined power of your own pieces, whilst diminishing the power of your opponent's pieces. Doing so enables you to choose from a wide range of moves, as more and more tactical opportunities become available to you. Possessing this superior power advantage makes it possible for you to exchange pieces until your opponent has no power left and is forced to concede defeat.

The true wonder of chess is that no matter who you play against, you are always facing your greatest opponent: <u>YOU</u>! While the degree of difficulty is largely determined by the ability of your opponent, the *real* battle is the inner game you play with yourself all throughout the entire duration of the game. Despite what the masses tend to believe, a game of chess consists of much more than merely the logical navigation of complex problems. For you to play to the very best of your ability, you must first overcome the struggle within you to successfully control your emotions. This is absolutely vital for you to be able to maintain concentration, replenish willpower and battle ferociously while staying calm and objective.

Since the dawn of warfare, force concentration has been an essential component of any military commander's repertoire. The good news is that you don't need to join the army in order to master the ability to concentrate fully. The truth is, however, that your success in every area of life will be mainly determined by your ability to win the "battles" that you encounter all throughout your life. These can be represented in the form of unpleasant challenges and painful setbacks you will inevitably face along the way.

In order for you to achieve any goal in life, whether it is a personal or professional one, you will need to concentrate your forces. The more complex and difficult the challenge is, the more important it will be to fully develop your ability to concentrate. Needless to say, this is infinitely easier said than done. Concentration involves converging all your strengths and skills together in order to maximise your personal power. Due to the unique balance of mental and emotional demands it requires, playing chess is the very best way to develop the power of concentration. Best of all, it is a game which is not only fun, but also provides never-ending lessons. These lessons can be easily applied in everyday life.

Concentration is much like mental adrenalin. In the same way that it would be physically harmful to be constantly engaged in fight-or-flight mode all the time, it would cause you extreme mental stress if you operated at maximum concentration all the time. In order to achieve your goals and ambitions, however, it is absolutely essential that you possess a well-developed ability to fully concentrate in crucial situations. Very often, your ability to maintain presence of mind will be the vital difference between success and failure.

Just like life itself, concentration is a form of self-mastery over time. Your mastery of chess, therefore, will correlate strongly with your mastery of life. While that might indeed seem to be a very bold claim, history provides countless examples of successful people, who attribute regularly playing chess to the attainment of their achievements.

Be warned that playing chess is very rarely a comfortable experience. For example, it is obviously *much* more relaxing to lounge on a sofa watching TV than it is to engage in hours of strenuous focus throughout a game of chess. This is especially the case if the level of your opponents requires that you are pushed to the max in order to defeat them. You <u>don't</u> play chess to have fun. Just like taking cold showers and doing barbell squats in the gym, the reason to regularly play chess is precisely *because* it is uncomfortable. Not only does it help you improve your ability to concentrate, it also helps you build mental fortitude.

Success in life is often achieved as a result of habitually confronting the challenging obstacles, which stand in front of you and your success. Constantly improving your chess-playing ability is best achieved by regularly playing opponents who are better than you. This will inevitably involve you losing sometimes, which is never a pleasant experience for your ego. Once you lose emotional attachment to the outcome of each game, however, you can focus on learning from your mistakes and becoming a more formidable challenge the next time you play the same opponent.

While you obviously play to win at all times, the true value you derive is what you learn, *not* whether you are declared the winner or loser of a single game. Do everything in your power to beat your opponents, of course. However, you will get the very most out of chess the moment you start viewing your opponents as people who are bringing out the very best in you by pushing you to the very limits of your mental capacity. Just like your body adapts to strenuous exercise workouts by getting fitter and stronger, chess greatly helps improve your mental capacity to plan ahead, evaluate others, anticipate responses and delay gratification. These are skills and habits which you will need to master in order to optimally nurture each of the 6 Dimensions Of Wellness.

There is a wonderful App available at Chess.com. Not only can you use it to improve your chess-playing ability, you can also connect with others worldwide and play against them. Another great way to improve your chess game is to join a local chess club. Compete against a wide variety of opponents; those who match you equally, those who are better than you, and those who you can easily beat. Provided you pay close attention to what insights you can take from each game of chess you play, you will learn from *everybody* you play, regardless of their level.

Spiritual

Mention the words "spiritual" and "spirituality" to some people and they may instinctively respond with a disapproving grimace or sigh. Sadly there is a very good reason for this. In recent times, spirituality has become big business. Consequently, self-appointed "experts" of all kinds have emerged in the global marketplace. In exchange for your hard-earned money, you are promised the solution to every single one of your problems. This is typically in the form of their books, seminars and online courses. The unfortunate reality is that these "experts" are the absolute *antithesis* of anything remotely spiritual in nature. If you've been cynical in the past, however, this chapter will hopefully help inspire you to both think and feel differently about all things spiritual.

Be Grateful For Gratitude!

I define "spiritual" as anything related to the human spirit or soul as opposed to material or physical things. Gratitude is an emotion expressing appreciation for what you already have in your life. A vital part of human evolution, it originated from the survival value of helping others and being helped in return. Research has demonstrated that there are specific areas of the brain that are involved in experiencing and expressing gratitude. From childhood to old age, increasing amounts of evidence are proving the wide array of psychological, physical, and relational benefits associated with deliberately cultivating gratitude as a daily habit.

The practice of gratitude is deeply ingrained in evolutionary history. It is a social emotion, which originated from the survival value of helping others and being helped in return. Many scientific studies have shown that there are areas of the brain that are specifically involved in experiencing and expressing gratitude.

Psychologists believe that feeling grateful is hugely beneficial for both physical and psychological health, especially among those who suffer from mental health problems. This is largely because practicing gratitude restricts the use of words expressing negative emotions or intentions. Instead, it directs inner attention away from negative emotions, including jealousy and resentment. This minimises the tendency to ruminate over such feelings, a common pattern that leads to deep unhappiness and depression. When the practice of gratitude is made an everyday habit, and is repeated over a long time, the physical benefits can be demonstrated by science. Brain scans show permanent changes in the prefrontal cortex of people who routinely express gratitude.

How To Practise Gratitude

Gratitude begins with simply observing and recognising the goodness in your life. It could be argued that prayer is the ultimate form of gratitude. Regardless of religion, however, gratitude is something which can be practised by everyone.

There are many people who warn against considering material possessions as sources of happiness. I would argue that it is a good thing to be grateful for what you already possess, provided your happiness *never* depends on owning things in the first place. Focus your sense of gratitude, therefore, on the more valuable things in life. Think about things which money simply can't buy. These would be your health and the relationships you have with your friends and family. In addition, you could also include recent insights and life lessons you have acquired.

The best way to practise gratitude is by keeping a daily gratitude journal. As with productivity, there are a wide range of apps available which you can use for this. I recommend you combine this with an old-fashioned gratitude journal, which you complete using your personal handwriting. This need not be anything fancy; a regular diary will do. The most important thing is <u>consistency</u>. Make it an everyday habit, like brushing your teeth before you go to bed every night. Doing so will help you break through any belief patterns which are holding you back. This process will guide you to a more empowered life filled with deeper meaning, enjoyment and appreciation.

The Importance Of Altruism

In both religious and secular societies, altruism is often perceived as being a supreme moral value. The word itself was first coined in the 19th century by French philosopher Auguste Comte. He defined altruism as "the elimination of selfish desire, as well as leading a life devoted to the well-being of others."

In the 21st century, however, few people believe altruism has a place in a world largely driven by competition and individualism. There *are* many fantastic aspects associated with individualism. Indeed, it cultivates a culture of initiative, creativity, and innovation. If left unchecked, however, it can very quickly lead to reckless selfishness and uncontrollable narcissism.

This would be to the detriment of mankind and is ultimately responsible for many of the problems we face today. Not only is the gap between the rich and the poor bigger than ever, many people who are affluent and seemingly "have it all" are actually more depressed than ever before.

When it comes to altruism, many believe it requires a big personal sacrifice, is too idealistic and offers no benefits to those who engage in such behaviour. The opposite is actually true. If you are seeking happiness and success, while remaining indifferent to others, you are unwittingly building an obstacle to your own happiness and success.

I believe that the single biggest cause of suffering in the Western World is our everyday obsession with loss and gain, pleasure and displeasure, praise and criticism, and fame and anonymity. This extreme way of thinking separates everything into being either "good" or "bad". All too often, this causes us to feel awful when we don't get what we want *when* we want.

By contrast, Eastern philosophies prioritise becoming better human beings by transforming their way of being and thinking. As a result, they feel infinitely more in control of circumstances and events. This makes it much less common for them to experience limiting emotions such as envy or feelings of inadequacy.

In the past, the main objects of admiration were "the wise". These were experienced and extraordinary men and women of unusual learning, judgment, or insight. They provided insights which enriched the lives of others. In current modern-day society, unfortunately, the famous and the rich have taken their place of "the wise". This has led to an overemphasis on accumulating wealth, materialistic goods and "achieving" fame. While none of these things are bad aspirations at all, they will never be enough all by themselves. This is because we ultimately gain the very highest degree of happiness and fulfilment when we first help *others*.

Making The Old Way Of Thinking New Again

You can often measure a culture's respect for the elderly in its language. In Hindi, for example, they use suffixes like '–ji' to refer to important individuals with an extra level of respect and recognition. Mahatma Gandhi, for instance, is often referred to as Gandhiji. In parts of Africa, younger speakers use the term 'mzee' to communicate a high level of respect for elders. In Hawaiian culture, kūpuna is the respectful term used for elders and is associated with knowledge, experience and expertise. Finally, the depth of Japan's deep regard for the elderly is reflected in their use of the suffix '-san'. Best of all is how the Japanese consider a person's 60th birthday. Known as Kankrei, it marks a rite of passage into old age and is considered to be a time for huge celebration.

In many areas of the Western World, unfortunately, the elderly are <u>not</u> treated with the respect they deserve. All too often, they are perceived as being senile and incompetent. Not only that, some cultures even go so far as to view see their elderly as a social *burden* and economic resource drain. A recent study showed a high rate of elderly suicides in France, in addition to a heat wave which killed 15,000 mostly elderly people. The French government responded by introducing Article 207 of the French Civil Code. Passed in 2004, it requires that adult children "keep in touch" with their elderly parents. It is a clear sign of how bad things have become when governments have to pass *laws* in order to force children to look after their parents.

This disconnect causes huge problems for society, not only for the elderly themselves, but for everyone else too. After all, we are *all* going to grow old. Therefore, we will all suffer as a result of this deeply flawed way of thinking and operating. The world's population is also getting older. People are now living longer than ever before, thanks to improvements in healthcare, nutrition and technology. Together with incredible new possibilities, this population shift also provides us with a whole new set of challenges. Doesn't it make sense, therefore, to improve our connection with the elderly and solve this problem <u>together</u> once and for all?

Volunteering - The Ultimate Connection Tool

There are many reasons why I recommend volunteering. It truly helps make a difference by helping those less fortunate than ourselves. But that's not the only benefit. When you volunteer, you will notice a subtle shift happening within yourself. Not only will you feel more connected to others, you will also become less absorbed in the normal stresses of daily life.

This is like an active form of mindfulness and gratitude combined. By shifting your focus to the needs of others, you simultaneously provide your mind with a much needed break from the various stresses in your life. This will result in you being recharged and eager to achieve even more of your goals. In addition, volunteering is an amazing way to connect with others and also contribute to your community. Not only do you connect with those who you help, you also build a deep connection with your fellow volunteers.

There are many worthy organisations which work tirelessly to help alleviate very complex problems. However, I recommend you choose an activity which enables you to see an immediate impact in terms of helping others. This will truly connect you to those whom you want to help, thus maximising the positive change you have on their lives. Based on my experiences, helping the aged is both the easiest and quickest way to help others in a powerful and profound way. As mentioned earlier in this chapter, disconnection from the elderly is a massive problem in Western society. Fortunately, it is a problem which is easily solved. Best of all, it is also lots of fun.

There are many ways in which you can volunteer. My preferred way is organising coffee events, through which I help introduce elderly men and women to each other. My intention is to help alleviate loneliness among the elderly community in Dublin. It is simple to organise and lots of fun to host. At the same time, it can actually be a truly life-changing experience for those who attend for the first time. This is because many of those who attend have totally lost connection with anything resembling a social life or even a circle of friends itself. Some are widows and widowers, whose whole lives revolved for so long around the companionship they shared with their partners. Without them, they find it extremely difficult to adapt and fill the void left by the deaths of their loved ones. Things that you take for granted, such as afternoon coffee events, can therefore be of *enormous* value to these people. Such events also serve as a great starting point when connecting with the elderly. Suggestions can be made, ideas can be exchanged and new initiatives can be launched from here.

Once you understand the importance of altruism, you will realise how much you will benefit from practising gratitude and regularly engaging in volunteering activities. As a result, your spiritual wellness will be at its peak and you will ultimately get much more out of life, especially in terms of a sense of happiness, satisfaction and overall well-being.

How Mindful Are You?

These days, you will hear a lot about how important mindfulness is. This is especially the case in this digital age of ever-advancing technology. Pause for a moment and consider how much the way you live is influenced, if not *controlled*, by technology. As wonderful as the Internet undoubtedly is, think about all the millions of people all around the world, whose lives mostly consist of a combination of text messages, Facebook posts, and Instagram selfies. Worst of all, it's very likely that you yourself own a mobile phone, which you carry around in your pocket every waking hour. If so, it is equally likely that you also check your phone countless times throughout the day to see if you have received any messages or if someone has "liked" one of your posts or photos on social media. If not, you can always count on your phone to *literally* alert you in the form of constant notification buzzes all throughout the day.

According to a 2010 Harvard study, your mind is not present with what you are doing for about half of your life, 47% of the time on average. Bearing in mind that we are now a full decade beyond when that study was conducted, my guess is that this percentage is even lower now. Rather than being tuned into the present, the masses instead waste way too much of their time either worrying, ruminating, judging, or even *obsessing* about things they couldn't ever possibly control in the first place.

Ahead of any other priority, both your brain and nervous system are wired to help you survive. Your brain is therefore on constant alert, scanning for threats and triggering the "flight or flight" stress response whenever it interprets danger. While this has worked impeccably well all throughout human history, this was only ever meant to occur on an occasional frequency. This is because, as mentioned earlier in this book, the "fight or flight" state stresses you both physically and psychologically to an enormous degree. Unfortunately, modern day living incurs various stresses on a daily basis, including many for which the human body is simply not designed to be able to handle. A perfect example would be the challenges facing corporate employees. Many are under constant pressure to achieve monthly sales targets and impress their bosses with presentations. At the same time, they worry about endless up-skilling, because they feel they will never be considered good enough otherwise. Add to this the fear of them losing their jobs and the subsequent catastrophic effect it would have on every single aspect of their lives.   If you can relate to any of this, you will benefit enormously from regularly practising mindfulness.

One of the best things about mindfulness is that it is incredibly simple and easy to learn. It is neither esoteric nor mysterious. Think of it as being exercise for the brain, through which you develop the ability to pay attention. There is no chanting or meditation involved and the results it generates are supported by many numerous experts in the field of neuroscience.

Since your neurobiology is designed to react quickly rather than to thoughtfully respond, you will instinctively tend to resist the unfamiliar. Instead, you will tend to remain safe within your familiar comfort zones. This is what causes you to automatically distance yourself from those who don't seem similar to you. While it may indeed be a natural thing to do, it doesn't exactly promote peace and harmony, let alone inspire new and exciting collaborations.

If constant distraction is the problem, then mindfulness is the solution. By exercising your brain, you learn how to pay attention to only that which is truly important. Rather than automatically and unconsciously drifting into autopilot mode, you will instead be fully present and "in the moment". This enriches all of your life experiences, whether it be you enjoying the food you eat on an entirely deeper level, or simply enjoying and appreciating the time you spend with loved ones. Once this happens, you will instantly realise that you were previously missing out on so many simple, yet amazing, things which life has to offer.

Imagine for a moment how much you would benefit if you could be present for even 10% more of your life.

How To Practise Mindfulness

There are two main ways to practise mindfulness:

1. Sit in silence and focus all of your attention on your breath as it moves in and out of your body. Every time you get distracted and you lose focus, you begin again and concentrate entirely on your breathing once again. With repeated practice, you will eventually develop the skill to totally immerse yourself in your breathing, "forgetting" about everything else for as long as your practice session lasts.

2. Engage in an everyday task, which is active and enables you to "lose yourself" in it. A perfect example would be tidying your house, a habitual action which causes you to engage your visual sense to an unusually heightened degree. The more you focus exclusively on the task of tidying, the more the rest of your senses are able to 'go on autopilot'. This is my preferred way to practise mindfulness because it ties in perfectly with the principles of connection covered in this book.

Gardening - The Ultimate Mindfulness Tool

Given the often evangelical promotion of mindfulness these days, it would easy to think of it as something modern that has only recently been discovered and developed. Not true!

Gardening, for example, has long been considered as an amazing way to achieve a sense of calm in an otherwise chaotic world. In fact, the Victorians had farms in the grounds of their mental health institutions, in which patients could experience the many positive psychological effects of gardening. These benefits were documented in a US study conducted back in 1798. Over the last 200 years, scientific research and evidence has backed up what gardeners have always known. One perfect example, for instance, is a study about the health and well-being benefits of allotment gardening. It was established that compared to the non-gardeners who participated in the study, the gardeners had better self-esteem and general health, combined with lower levels of fatigue and depression.

Much like mindfulness, gardening connects you to the world around you, enriching your life with peace and pleasure in the most profound ways possible. This is exactly what nature is designed to do, one of its fundamental functions. As human beings, the act of working the soil is literally and metaphorically *ingrained* in our entire evolution and psyche. This is why someone who has never gardened before can instantly find familiarity, comfort and pleasure in tending to plants and the earth. This has certainly been the case for me.

Foodscaping

One of the reasons I recommend gardening as a form of mindfulness is because of the opportunities it provides you to connect with other like-minded people. Foodscaping is best described as being a hybrid between gardening and farming. The eventual aim of it is to create an all-encompassing way of growing a garden, feeding yourself, and achieving the peace of mind that accompanies the entire process. Instead of grass and shrubberies, it involves growing plants, which yield fruits and vegetables.

Everyone has the space to grow something edible. Even if you do not have a garden, you can use a windowsill to grow herbs and vegetables. Recognising that many people do not have much garden space, seed and plant merchants are continually working on breeding new varieties, which are more suitable for pot-growing.

Rather than trying to grow everything by yourself and *for* yourself, however, I recommend using foodscaping as a means to connect with others. For example, I have recently started a foodscaping collective with some of my local neighbours. We grow different plants to each other and then arrange regular meetings. Here, we exchange what we've grown with each other. Everyone involved enjoys the process of growing the plants from seed and eating the fresh food we have collectively harvested. Most of all, we enjoy and value the friendships we have created through engaging in foodscaping together.

When you become engrossed in foodscaping, it causes you to direct all of your attention toward your inner experience, toward others, and toward the environment around you. It also creates a mindset which is fully open, compassionate, receptive, and accepting of others. Together with the beehive analogy described at the beginning of this book, foodscaping is the perfect metaphor for the Connection Code."

Want to become part of the Tribe Shift Foodscaping Collective? Email me at paul@tribeshift.com

Vocational

*"If one advances confidently in the
direction of his dreams, and
endeavours to live the life which
he has imagined, he will
meet with a success unexpected
in common hours."*

This is a quote taken from "Walden" by Henry David Thoreau. It is most frequently used to recommend following one's passion and ultimately achieving a life of extraordinary success and fulfilment as a result of doing so. Very few people live and act according to this belief though. Trapped by their fear of failure and what other people think, they live "lives of quiet desperation" according to Thoreau. To reach your chosen destination, however, you will *need* to choose the road less travelled. This road will inevitably involve you having to encounter and overcome all the obstacles and challenges involved along the way.

Choose Your Hero's Journey

Human beings are impatient creatures of comfort. We instinctively and instantly look for the quickest and easiest option, one which involves the minimum amount of time, effort and pain. Rather than always avoiding discomfort, however, it is often a good idea to view every challenging situation as an opportunity to evolve. After all, history provides us with countless examples of how high achievers turned adversity into success, thanks to the power of perception, action and will.

Whether or not they are consciously aware of it, all high achievers understand that happiness comes from solving problems. It is hardly as if they never had problems in the first place. In fact, most high achievers *attribute* their success to the trauma they experienced in childhood, together with the seemingly insurmountable obstacles they had to overcome along the way before ultimately achieving their extraordinary level of success.

Instead of avoiding your problems, therefore, <u>actively seek them out</u> and be *grateful* for the opportunities they present you. Use all the pain from your past as fuel to create the future you desire and deserve. In order to overcome the many inevitable obstacles blocking the way to your success, you will be forced to evolve into a much better version of yourself in the process. This journey of personal growth is a constant work-in-progress, which never ever ends. Finding the solutions to the problems of today will always lead you to a better tomorrow.

In order for you to achieve your goals in life, you will be regularly faced with obstacles. These will range from difficult challenges to extreme adversity. To overcome adversity, you must care about something so much that you're willing to do everything that is required to overcome it. To find such a degree of infinite motivation and desire, you must first identify your Hero's Journey.

Created by academic Joseph Campbell in 1949, The Hero's Journey is a classic story structure that's featured in countless stories from all over the world. In each of the tales, the characters each set out on their adventures to get what they need, face conflict, and ultimately triumph over adversity.

There are 3 stages of the Hero's Journey:

The Departure Act: the Hero leaves the Ordinary World.
The Initiation Act: the Hero ventures into unknown territory
("Special World") and becomes a true champion through various trials and challenges.

The Return Act: the Hero returns in triumph.

Films such as Star Wars, Rocky and The Matrix are clear examples of movies which use the Hero's Journey story structure. All 3 movies involve unlikely heroes, who have to overcome their doubts and undergo tremendous transformations throughout their journey. This personal growth is crucial to them succeeding, in spite of incredible adversity. As a result, they are able to triumphantly return as the heroes they have become.

Despite all of these stories being fictional, the story of your own life works in exactly the same way. In order to achieve your personal and professional goals, you will have to constantly overcome adversity in a wide variety of forms. Through doing so, you will transform yourself into the hero of your own story. The first step is to uncover and identify the final destination on your Hero's Journey, i.e. the achievement of your dream. For this to happen, you require this vital component: clarity

The Path Made Clear

If a pond is clouded with mud, there's nothing that can be done to make the water clear. Once you allow the mud to settle, however, it will clear all by itself, because clarity is the water's natural state. In much the same way, clarity is also your mind's natural state.

When you have a clear head, you are able to perform to the very best of your ability. You know exactly what do, at exactly the right time, and exactly how to do it perfectly. Compare this to when you are nervous and your mind is consumed with a multitude of fears, worries and anxieties. It is only when you've got absolutely *nothing* on your mind that you're then free to function at your very best.

Clarity allows you to be present in the moment. This provides you with a sense of purpose, direction and the entrepreneurial spirit, which is an absolutely crucial requirement for maximum achievement in life.

Every person is born with clarity. What "muddies the water" is an amalgamation of fears and limiting beliefs, which are installed into our minds early into our childhoods. Regaining clarity is simply a matter of emptying your mind of these fears and limiting beliefs, whilst simultaneously filling your heart full of joy. You achieve this by finding your tribe. This is the continuous process of upgrading your peer group so that you <u>only</u> surround yourself with people who respect you, value you and will constantly help you move towards the achievement of all your goals. As well as this, you *must* do what you love and *love* what you do.

While you may not currently be able to turn your passion into a full-time career, begin your Hero's Journey NOW by surrounding yourself with the kind of people who will help you transform into the hero you need to become. Creating an environment in which you will thrive and grow is an incredibly significant first step on your journey towards greatness. Not only does it hugely benefit your emotional wellness, it also motivates and inspires you to take optimum care of the other 4 dimensions of your wellness: Physical, Spiritual, Social and Intellectual.

Once you choose to follow your heart's calling, your mind will instantly begin to clear. As this happens, the path on which you begin your Hero's Journey will suddenly present itself to you.

Connect all 6 dimensions of wellness
Connect with your purpose
Connect with others

Ultimately, it is only <u>fear</u> which is preventing you from pursuing your dreams, ambitions and aspirations. This fear is in the form of limiting beliefs, which have you believing that you either don't know enough, or that what you dream about isn't actually possible in the first place. Both of these beliefs are absolute bullshit!

You didn't always think in this way. When you were a child, you were at the height of your creative powers. You believed everything was possible. You followed your heart and everything was fun, playful and packed full of joy. It was only when you were told by others that you couldn't or shouldn't do something that fear and doubt entered your head.

When you follow your head instead of your heart, the direction of your life is determined by the limiting beliefs which keep you paralysed by fear. Consequently, you don't ever pursue the ideal life you originally imagined and your dreams forever remain unrealised fantasies.

This flawed way of thinking that you are somehow "not enough" is rife within the Western world. This message is constantly broadcasted through television and social media. The message is that you are not rich enough, not good-looking enough and not famous enough. All of this bullshit distracts you from accepting and loving yourself and others. It prevents you from getting the very most out of life.

None of this ever happens within indigenous tribes. In this environment, there is absolutely no concept of flaws and weaknesses. Instead, everyone is unconditionally respected, appreciated and valued. In the same ways that bees work together in harmony for the benefit of the hive, all of the members use their unique strengths and habits to benefit the others within the tribe.

The Sat Nav Of Success

Imagine what would happen if you applied this way of thinking to the way you live. Then, ask yourself this:

"What would you do if you had all the money in the world and you knew you couldn't fail?"

This is my very favourite question to ask a person. Since it is the first time they are likely to have been asked this, their initial response always intrigues me. As they attempt to answer it, you can almost see the cogs running in their brain as they try to separate reality (the ways things currently are) from fantasy (the way they wish things could be in the future). Doing so involves them temporarily abandoning all of their limiting beliefs. These are the beliefs which are currently preventing them from even *trying* to move in the direction of their goals, let alone actually achieving them.

Answering this question is crucial in terms of establishing your current level of vocational wellness. It also helps provide you with the direction you need in order to live the life you want. It is vital to understand that there never *is* any end "destination" you ever reach. The reward is the journey, together with the friends and connections you make along the way. You also become the best version of yourself in the process.

This is really the entire point of the journey itself in the first place.

The Meaning Of Life?

The further you are removed from the life you would ideally live, the more unhappy and unsatisfied you will be. The closer you move towards the life of your dreams, the happier and more satisfied you will be. It all sounds so simple, yet very few people actually behave in accordance to this fundamental truth.

If the very thought of chasing your dreams overwhelms you completely, you're already on the right track! Your goals *should* be so big that they seem impossible. They are meant to be exactly like that. Achieving your goals will require you to face your fears, go where it is uncomfortable, and achieve an incredible personal transformation because of all of this.

If you don't know how to even start, don't worry. Once you have found your why, you will figure out the how, who, what and where involved. Imagine as if your brain operates exactly like a satellite navigation system. Choose your destination, which is your "ideal life". I recommend you base it around the 6 Dimensions Of Wellness outlined in this book.

When it comes to achieving your goals, your success will be directly linked to your ability to connect with other people. To achieve your friendship and relationship goals, for example, the very best way to do this is by expanding your social network. Doing this will significantly increase the range of options and opportunities available to you.

Business provides the very best example of the value of cooperation with others. To become successful in your entrepreneurial ventures, your progress will be made possible by hiring or collaborating with those whose strengths are your weaknesses. Recruiting such individuals will enable you to spend your time playing to your strengths and doing what you do best. This will greatly accelerate your progress. It will also prevent you from experiencing excess stress and frustration.

When selling and marketing your products and services, your success will be determined by your ability to effectively connect with customers. This is the essence of what is known as "relationship marketing". The stronger the connections you make, the stronger your business will become. Best of all, your happy customers will be delighted to refer you new business by introducing you to their connections.

Social

The Importance Of Having A Great Social Life

Connecting with others has always been something which comes naturally to me. I love meeting new people and always make a conscious and continuous effort to do. While people often see networking as a necessary evil in the form of a mundane business practice, I connect with everyone on a personal level first and foremost. I never give any thought whatsoever as to what I can "get" as a result of interacting with someone. Instead, I lead with warmth, positivity and good intentions. I trust that the connections I make will result in things going exactly the way they are meant to go. I might make a new friend. I might make a useful business contact. I might even have a pleasant (or unpleasant) conversation with someone whom I may never speak to again. It's all good to me. Regardless of the eventual outcome, I make a connection of some kind.

Once you adopt a "paying it forward" philosophy, you will immediately experience the benefits of doing so. Not only does this introduce a sense of abundance, it simply makes life much more enjoyable. Simply put, it is nice to be nice.

Connection is made easy once you adopt the approach of helping yourself as a result of first helping others. You will feel infinitely more relaxed when attempting to connect with others, regardless of their actual response. Always be aware that when you approach someone with good intentions and are treated unkindly, it reveals a lot about their insecurities, not any of your faults. Be grateful that such individuals are immediately disqualifying themselves from being people with whom you wish to associate. Your vibe will always attract your tribe. Only associate with those who will help improve your life. In return, you will also help improve their lives, however and whenever you can. As with everything in life, balance is always the key.

I have found that the very best way to connect with others is by organising social events. Through them, I make new connections and deepen connections I have already made. Social events are merely a way to initiate connections. It is not merely a way to make new friends however. Businesses of all kinds, for example, require the connection of their products and services to their clients and customers. That is the whole point of advertising and marketing in the first place. Making 1-2-1 connections on a personal level, however, speeds things up greatly. Regardless of your wants and needs on a personal or professional level, connection is always the key.

The most vital ingredient for connection is intimacy. Unfortunately, society has conditioned people to only associate the word intimacy with sex. It is truly <u>so</u> much more. Intimacy is essentially about knowing yourself and being known by others for who you *really* are in every single area of your life. The best way to do this is to focus on improving each of the 6 Dimensions Of Wellness and connecting with others while you do so. You will form close bonds as you work together to help each other achieve your individual and collective goals.

Join A Special Interest Group

The quickest way to expand your social circle is by attending events organised and hosted by others. The best website for regular events happening locally is MeetUp. This is an online service used to create groups that host local in-person events. There are approximately 35 million Meetup users worldwide. The site's events are a fantastic way for you to make new friends, share a hobby, and expand your network of contacts. No matter how unique you believe your interests are, you will find others on MeetUp who share them and who want to meet people just like you. It's a simple yet powerful way to quickly bond with others, many of whom may end up becoming good friends of yours.

Accept The Social Challenge

Once you have discovered the benefits of attending social events, the next step to take is to organise events of your own.   If you seem reluctant to accept this challenge, that's all the more reason to do it! Organising and hosting events regularly will challenge you in ways that will force you to grow in a very positive way. This will bring out the very best in you. As a result, you will make many personal and professional contacts that you would not make otherwise.

The biggest benefit of events is that they provide you the opportunity to improve your wellness in each of the 6 dimensions covered in this book. It therefore makes sense to attend and organise events based around each of these dimensions. Use events to connect with others, whilst simultaneously improving your physical, emotional, spiritual, intellectual, vocational and social wellness.

Cracking The Connection Code

If you've been trying to do everything all by yourself, is it any wonder why you often feel inadequate, overwhelmed and alone? There has never been anything wrong with you. You've simply failed to realise that you needed the help and cooperation of *other* people to help you on your journey.

Imagine an entire community of people with all the skills, resources and contacts you could ever possibly need to achieve all of your personal and professional goals. Then imagine that all you ever needed to do to receive all of this help was to simply use your unique set of skills, resources and contacts to help others.

This is essentially how indigenous tribes of all types and forms operate. Nobody within a tribe ever feels inadequate or stressed out because of their weaknesses. This is because they are so busy having fun using their strengths to help others. This is exactly what builds and maintains the sense of harmony, balance and connection within tribes.

Human beings have always been precisely designed to co-exist with each other. Over the centuries, the advent of colonialism has resulted in fear and greed infecting the mindsets of those living within non-tribal cultures. The erroneous notion of being separate from others has created a horrible sense of disconnection. This is the root cause of feelings of depression, stress, anxiety, inadequacy, loneliness and isolation. Connection is the only solution to this problem.

The Way Forward

When we think of what the world is, we tend to think it is the same thing as planet Earth, a huge landmass with a population of nearly 7.5 billion people. *Your* world, however, actually consists of the people who are part of your life. This typically includes your family, friends, work colleagues, customers, clients or casual acquaintances. In the past, your world was determined and limited by your geographic location. Today, you have the Internet. In the form of a mobile phone, you have the ultimate connection tool. It enables you to connect with like-minded people, who share similar interests, values and goals. These people can be located locally or scattered all over the planet. Basically, you can essentially create your *own* world by connecting with the right people.

My online community, Tribe Shift, works to help members with their personal and professional development. As a member, the more you work to help other members, the more you are rewarded in terms of opportunities and exposure through the website, blog, podcast and social media channels. This means the opportunity available is the same for every member of the community, regardless of gender, race, religion, sexuality or socioeconomic background. It is the ultimate form of "paying it forward". The more you give, the more you get. I look forward to connecting there and applying all of the principles contained in this book together.

To find out more, go to www.tribeshift.com

Printed in Great Britain
by Amazon

78120659R00068